The Ultimate Profit Improvement Guide for Tradespeople

By Kirsten Hawke C.A.

We understand the long hours, physical challenges and paperwork struggles that tradespeople face today so we have developed this guide packed with strategies, templates and calculators to show you how to increase your profit and make more money.   Whether you are an owner operator or larger trade firm you will find solutions and tips to help.

To subscribe to our newsletter mailing list visit
www.tradeaccountant.co.nz

This book is dedicated to my wonderful husband Dave and awesome children Alex and Brianna. You rock my world!!

Table of Contents

What is Profit?

Marketing

    The Ten Minute Marketing Formula

    Testimonials

    Follow up calls

    Database

    Lead Generation

Systems and Software

    Systems Manual

    Accounting

    CRM

    Job management

    Payroll

    Get paid on time

    Terms of trade

Understanding the Numbers

      Get pricing right

      Discounting

      Know your breakeven point

      Gross Profit

      Mark up vs margin

      Benchmarking

      KPIs

Team

About the author

Resources and References

What is profit?

Profit is what's left over after you've paid all your expenses. It's the result of what happens to and in your business. It is the best measure of your business success.

You have control over some, but not all, of the factors that control profit.

This book shows you how to control the four factors that determine your profit and use them to create increased profitability.

The four factors are:

1. The price you charge for your products and/or services.

2. The quantity (or volume) of products and/or services you sell.

3. The costs you incur directly in producing or buying the products and services you sell. These are called variable costs because they increase and decrease as your sales increase or decrease.

4. Those costs you incur whether you make any sales or not. They are best described as fixed costs because they do not change in sales volume, at least not on a day-to-day basis.

Lets start with the quantity (or volume) of sales.

The main driver of this is marketing.

Marketing for tradespeople

One of the things that most business people overlook is that effective marketing doesn't have to be complicated or expensive to do.

A few minutes each day spent doing some simple things can produce some remarkable results.

And that's the purpose of the Ten Minute Marketing Programme developed by Graham McGregor. Graham McGregor is a marketing consultant and the creator of the 396 page Free 'Unfair Business Advantage Report.' www.theunfairbusinessadvantage.com.

This simple marketing system has helped many businesses to grow their revenues by 10% or more over a 12 month period.

Best of all it only takes ten minutes a day to do.

Here's how it works:

Look at the following marketing chart.

Your goal is to do a minimum of four marketing activities each day from this chart.

Send out one thank you card	Give away one business card
Make a follow up phone call to one person	Ask one person for a referral

Now you can combine these marketing activities any way you like each day.

So you could send out two thank you cards today and also make two follow up phone calls.

Or maybe you could do one activity from each box.

The goal though is to do a minimum of four marketing activities every work day.

Now four marketing activities a day is close to 1,000 extra marketing activities a year.

That's a lot of extra marketing activities each year and is the reason why businesses that use this system increase their revenues by 10% or more over 12 months.

Let me give you some detailed information on how to use each of these marketing activities in your trade business.

Ten Minute Marketing Strategy One:

Thank You Cards

Thank you cards are a wonderful way to quickly get large numbers of people eager to talk about your trade services to many of the people they know.

A thank you card is just a small card that has the words **Thank You** printed on the front. The inside of the card is blank so you can write your own handwritten message.

Here's how Thank You Cards work.

Each work day all you have to do is send out between two and four thank you cards. So if you work five days a week you will be sending out between 10 and 20 thank you cards each week.

That might not sound a lot, but 10 thank you cards a week is around 500 thank you cards in a year.

In each thank you card that you send out it's important you write a short 3-4 sentence **HANDWRITTEN** message. Why do you hand write a message?

Let me ask you an important question:

How many handwritten thank you cards have you received from anyone in business over the last twelve months?

I've asked hundreds of business people this question and the average number of handwritten thank you cards they've received is two or less in a whole year.

So when you start sending out thank you cards with a handwritten message inside them people will remember your business very positively. Because so few people take the time to do something like this.

There are many occasions where thank you cards are very useful. Here are some of these occasions and the words you could write when you send out each thank you card.   More examples are available in our Easy Profits for Tradepeople Ebook   FREE   to   newsletter   subscribers   at www.tradeaccountant.co.nz/

1.   Thank you card after a phone contact

"Hi Bob; thank you for your time on the phone today. I enjoyed talking with you and look forward to sharing some interesting ideas with you shortly.   Regards John."

On this occasion you may have spoken to a potential new trade client on the phone and have made an appointment to see them for a meeting.

This thank you card thanks them for their time on the phone and lets them know they will hear some interesting ideas when you meet.

Notice that the thank you card is only a few sentences long. One of the things I love about thank you cards is that they are so quick to write.

Important Point:

Make sure you always enclose one of your business cards with every thank you card you send out.

2. Thank you card after a meeting with a potential trade client.

"Hi Bob; thank you for the opportunity to discuss your project. I look forward to talking with you again soon. Regards John"

In case you are wondering it is perfectly acceptable to send multiple thank you cards to the same person.

You can send one after a phone contact, one after a first meeting or presentation and so on.

Multiple thank you cards have a wonderfully positive impact on the people you send them to.

One of the reasons that handwritten notes work much better than thank you notes by email is that handwritten thank you cards in business have almost disappeared today.

So if you send one you are immediately noticed as being different from most other people in business.

3. Thank you card after a trade sale

"Hi Bob; thank you for choosing my services. I know you will be delighted with the wonderful job we do and look forward to your positive feedback. Regards John."

A very common experience when you buy any product or service (particularly one that costs a lot of money) is what we call 'Buyer's Remorse".

In other words you wonder if you've made the right decision buying this product or service.

A thank you card after a client purchase goes a long way toward reducing any second thoughts or doubts they may have about what they have bought.

It's also nice to be thanked for spending money with a business. In over 95% of situations where you spend money on product or service you never receive a hand written thank you for becoming a client.

So sending a thank you card means you are immediately remembered.

4. Thank you card to a person who gives you a referral

"Hi Bob; thanks for the referral to Fred Smith. I appreciate your thoughtfulness. I'll let you know how I get on when I talk with him. Regards John."

If you want more referrals from your trade clients to other people they know it pays to thank them when they do give a referral to you. This short thank you card does just that. The more you thank people for referrals the more likely they are to give you more referrals. And we all want more referrals because they are so easy to talk with and are very likely to become clients as well.

5: Thank you card to a person who gives you a referral updating them on the result:

'Hi Bob, just wanted to let you know I had a good discussion with Fred Smith today about our services. Fred is interested in what we do and there is a good chance that he may want to use our services in the near future. I'll let you know if that happens. Thanks again for the referral to Fred. I appreciate it. Regards John".

Letting people know how you got on with the referral they gave you is a really nice thing to do.

And it's so easy to do as well.

For more examples sign up for the free EBook at www.tradeaccountant.co.nz.

Final Comment on Thank You Cards:

As you can see, there are lots of different occasions to send out thank you cards.

I encourage you to get into the regular habit of sending out at least 2-4 handwritten thank you cards each work day.

It will be one of the smartest things you ever do if you want to get large numbers of new clients along with some great repeat and referral business.

Where do you get thank you cards from?

You can buy thank you cards from the greeting card section in most major book and stationery stores. You can also get your local digital printer to print them for you. (That's what I do.)

Ten Minute Marketing Strategy Two:

Follow up phone calls

These are very simple to make yet very few businesses actually make them.

There are two types of follow up phone calls you can make. You can make them to existing trade clients or customers and you can make them to potential trade clients or customers.

A follow up phone call should be short, friendly, positive and low key.

A follow up phone call could be as simple as you ringing up a client and saying '*Hi it's John here from XYZ here. Just a quick call to say thanks again for being a client and that everything is going well for you?*'

If your client or customer is not available when you phone, just leave a polite and friendly message on their phone.

Say something like this:

"*Hi Mary, its John here from XYZ here. We like to add value and stay in touch with our clients. This is just a quick call to make sure you are still enjoying the work we did for you recently. If we can be of any further help you can contact us on 1234-5678. Thanks again for being a client. Your name.*"

Follow up phone calls to existing clients are a classy way to show them you value their business.

And with at least 10% of follow up calls your customers will often mention an opportunity for a repeat purchase or talk about someone they know who could be interested in buying the types of things you sell.

Follow up phone calls are very easy to make to potential clients or customers as well. These are usually people who have already contacted your business and expressed an interest in your trade services They haven't yet purchased so it's worth while to stay in touch with them on a regular basis.

Just think of a good reason to phone potential clients.

It could be something like this...

'Hi Mary, it's John here from XYZ here. You might recall we had a chat a few days ago our services. I thought I'd give you a quick call because I've just had some very interesting feedback from two clients who used our services recently for a similar type of project to what you have in mind. Can I send you details of what these clients thought of our services?"

The good news is that there is always some sort of reason to phone a potential client or customer and give them some sort of helpful information.

And you'll be amazed at how often a simple follow up call like this will create brand new business for you.

Ten Minute Marketing Strategy Three:

Asking for referrals

This is free and when you do it correctly you can get dozens of good referrals to speak to every month.

When you ask for referrals I recommend you try something like this...

"Hi John, I wonder if you could help me? Who are two or three people you know who might be interested in interested in using the services of a professional tradesperson. Who would you suggest I send some information to?"

Now a question like this is very low key and friendly. You are just asking a person for the names of several people that might be interested in receiving some helpful information about your services. This makes it very easy for a person to give you a few people to talk to.

I've discovered that when you ask for two or three people you will often get two people as referrals.

If you ask for one or two people as referrals you will often get one person as a referral.

Why not try asking for six or seven?

So asking for referrals is well worth trying in your trade business. And well worth practising until you get good at it.

Ten Minute Marketing Strategy Four:

Giving away business cards

This is often overlooked. Make it a point to give away business cards on a regular basis to many of the people you come in contact with.

Say something like this when you hand them out:

'Hi my name is John and I'm a professional tradesperson. If you come across someone who might be interested getting an outstanding trade job done, feel free to give them one of my business cards."

A key rule in all marketing is that "you never know who someone knows."

So someone you meet at a coffee lounge on a casual basis could easily refer you to someone who could be a great customer for your services.

So give away business cards on a regular basis.

Summary:

We've covered some very simple marketing strategies in the Ten Minute Marketing Programme.

Let's go through them one more time...

Remember this marketing chart?

Your goal is to do a minimum of four marketing activities each day from this chart.

Send out one thank you card	Give away one business card
Make a follow up phone call to one person	Ask one person for a referral

Now you can combine these marketing activities any way you like each day.

So you could send out two thank you cards today and also make two follow up phone calls.

Or maybe you could do one activity from each box.

The goal though is to do a minimum of four marketing activities every work day.

And when you do this on a regular basis you'll get some exciting results with very little effort.

Let's take a look now at Testimonials.

Positive Client Testimonials

I learned a simple but important marketing rule many years ago...

I call this marketing rule **The McGregor Rule of Ten.**

The McGregor Rule of Ten says:

What other people say about you, your company, your products and services is at least **ten times more credible** than anything you can say on your own behalf:

In other words:

- If you say it, potential clients and customers will tend to doubt what you say.
- If your existing customers say it, the same thing is far more believable

You see the **McGregor Rule of Ten** in action when someone you know says to you: *'You should use this business because they are very good.'*

And this simple word of mouth recommendation is usually far more effective at getting you to become a new customer than this same business spending a huge amount of money on a glossy four colour brochure, a large Yellow Pages advertisement or a fancy website.

This is an obvious marketing strategy yet only a tiny number of businesses actually use it.

So your goal is to collect some great written testimonials from some of your best trade clients.

You want these testimonials to say what they like about your trade services, the benefits they have got from using your services and the reasons why they would recommend your trade services to other people they know.

So how do you get great written testimonials that say all these things?

Just follow these simple steps.

Step One: Identify several dozen trade clients who you know really like your trade services.

Step Two: Send these clients a short letter that says something like this.

Mary, I wonder if you could do me a small favour.

I'm often talking to new clients about them using my services. It would really be helpful if I could show these people some feedback from people like you who have already used my services.

I've enclosed a very simple one page client feedback form that has a few brief questions on it.

Would you mind taking a couple of minutes to answer these questions and then send the form back to me?

I've enclosed a stamped addressed envelope for your convenience and you are welcome to fax it back as well if that's more convenient.

I know your time is valuable so I have a free $5 Lotto Ticket I'd like to give you for taking the time to do this. Just send this form back in the next 7 days and I'll send this free Lottery Ticket out to you.

Thanks again if you are able to help me.

Your Name

Step Three: With this letter you also attach a very simple one page client feedback form that will give you the type of testimonials you are looking for.

The Client Feedback Form looks like this.

Client Feedback Form for XYZ Trade Services:

Please send this form back to XYZ Trade Services at (Your postal Address) or feel free to fax it back to (Your fax number.) I have a free $5 Lottery Ticket if you can do this by (Put in a date seven days from now.)

Question One: What are three things you like most about using our services?

1

2

3

Question Two: What are three benefits you've received from using our services?

1

2

3

Question Three: What are three reasons why you would recommend our services to other people you know?

1

2

3

Question Four: Can we use some of your comments in our marketing? Yes (...) No (...)

When you send out this short letter and one page client feedback form always enclose a stamped addressed envelope. You do this to make it very easy for your clients to send the form back. That's also why you offer the option of returning it by fax.

If you send this letter and client feedback form out to 10-20 of your best clients around 20% or more will complete this form and send it back to you.

Obviously you then send them their free Lottery Ticket along with a thank you card that says

"Mary, thanks for your positive feedback. It was very useful and I appreciate it. Your Name."

Step Three: All you then do is use your computer to write down whatever answers they give you and put their name at the bottom. Bingo, you now have some great client testimonials.

Use a heading something like this:

"Here are some comments from our clients on why they like using XYZ Tradespeople."

"What I really like about XYZ Tradespeople is 1,2,3. The benefits I've received from using XYZ Tradespeople are 4,5,6. The reasons why I'd recommend XYZ Tradespeople to other people is 7,89 " **Client Name.**

Here's what this would look like:

"What I really like about XYZ Tradespeople is that they show up exactly on time and are always neat and tidy. They helped me transform the look of a house I had for sale and did it quickly and with a smile. I'd recommend them because they are professional, friendly and extremely knowledgeable." **Mary Brown.**

How do you use these client testimonials?

You should include them with every trade quote you give. You can put them on your website. You can use them anytime someone asks you *"Why should I use your trade services?"*

All you do is say something like this:

'That's a great question. Here is some recent feedback from some of my trade clients that gives some interesting answers to this question. Let me show you what they have to say." And then show this person some of your positive testimonials. Positive testimonials from happy trade clients are literally worth their weight in gold.

Action Plan

Start collecting a few today.

Sign up to our newsletter at www.tradeaccountant.co.nz and receive a FREE copy of the Solid Gold Testimonials Marketing Guide (within 24 hours) written by Graham McGregor.

Use Digital Photos as well:

I also suggest you take a few digital photos of every trade job you do. Take photos before, during and after each job. And then use these photos in all your marketing. So if you have a client that is thinking of hiring you to add a deck to the outside of their home, show this client a number of before and after digital photos of other clients where you have added a deck to their home. A picture really is worth a thousand words.

And the good news about photos is that in most cases you can show great results from your services. So use digital photos as another simple marketing tool to show potential new clients how good your services are.

Now let's take a look at follow up.

The 30 Day Added Value Follow Up

This is ridiculously simple to do, yet no one does it.

Just take three simple action steps with every new trade client you get.

Step One:

Send them a short hand written thank you card thanking them for their business. We've covered this earlier in the Ten Minute Marketing Strategy.

Step Two:

A few days after you have done the work for your new client send them a small unexpected gift.

This could be a couple of free movies passes, a small pot plant, a positive book or anything at all you think will make them feel valued.

Include with this gift a short thank you card that has a message something like this.

"Mary thanks again for becoming a new client. I appreciate your business and thought you might enjoy this small gift. With my compliments. Regards Your Name."

Let me ask you another question.

When was the last time anyone you know received a small unexpected gift from anyone in business including trades people?

It's extremely rare and virtually never happens.

So when you give a small gift you position your trade business as being special and different.

Doing this shows you really care about your clients.

Step Three:

A few days after you send out a small gift you take two minutes and make a quick follow up phone call.

You might say something like this:

"Hi Mary, just a quick call to make sure that you are really enjoying the job we did for you?"

You then have a brief chat and then politely end the call. What you are demonstrating here is that you really do care about your clients because it is extremely unusual to get a follow up call from any tradesperson.

With this 30 Day Added Value Follow Up you have shown that your trade business is special. You add a lot of value to your clients. You thank them, you appreciate their business and you take the time to make sure everything you did they are happy with.

In short you've made yourself the ideal builder for them to happily recommend to everyone they know.

You are special, you are different and you are a great choice for anyone that wants to use a builder. All this from putting into place a very simple 30 Day Added Value follow up programme.

The Three Tradespeople marketing strategies I've now covered are very easy to do.

However they will only work if you actually use them.

Action Plan

1: Use the ten minute marketing formula in your trade business each work day. Just do four simple marketing activities and over a year that is 1,000 extra marketing activities you are now doing.

Do this consistently and you'll be delighted at the great results this will produce in new sales for your trade business.

2: Collect some great trade testimonials using the very simple client feedback form and cover letter above.

3: Sign up to our newsletter at www.tradeaccountant.co.nz and receive a FREE copy of the Solid Gold Testimonials Marketing Guide (within 24 hours) written by Graham McGregor.

4. Then use these positive testimonials in all your marketing.

Positive testimonials are one of the easiest ways I know to prove how good you are and to get large numbers of new clients eager to use your services.

Use digital photos as well.

5: Delight your new trade clients with a simple **30 Day Added Value follow up programme.**

Send them a hand written thank you card, give them a small unexpected present and make a quick follow up phone call.

This will give you huge amounts of both repeat and referral business when you do it on a regular basis.

The real secret to all business success is that at some point you have to **TAKE ACTION**

Now let's take a look at your database.

Contact your database

Keeping in contact with your database is the cheapest and easiest way to increase your sales.

Send your customers a regular newsletter with helpful tips.

Below is an example for Electricians:

Start with a holiday newsletter "Ten things to do to protect your home before going on holiday"

Tip One: could be making sure the mail is cleared by a neighbour.

Tip Six: could be use a timer switch to make sure your home looks occupied.

Tip Nine: could be unplug all your appliances

Tip Ten: Contact us for any outstanding electrical work.

Go to http://blog.business-buddy.co.nz/tip-sheets/ to view one we have put together for Electricians. Feel free to use this as a template for your tip sheet.

Think about offering your customers holiday deals – offer them something for free – this can be an item of high value to them and low cost to you– maybe free light bulbs/smoke detectors/batteries with any work completed before Christmas.

If you don't have a database that is easy to manage look on-line there are many different options.

Now let's take a look at Lead Generation.

Lead Generation

It's really important to have marketing gravity.

Have at least 10 different lead generation systems in place every month.

Here are some examples:

Have a referral system in place – reward and thank your customers for any referrals they make.

Ask your clients for referrals.

Join a networking group such as BNI.

Make sure your website is up to date, relevant and easy to use.

Invest in Google adwords.

Use other peoples networks. Run offers in conjunction with other firms

Nurture relationships with compatible businesses, e.g. with real estate agents. Present your services to these groups e.g. at your local Real Estate office team meetings.

Make a list of your ideal customers and create a marketing plan to suit.

Action Plan

Decide on 10 lead generation systems and implement at least one a week for the next 10 weeks.

Lead Generator	By Whom	By When
1		
2		
3		
4		
5		
6		
7		
8		
9		
10		

Systems and Software

Well run businesses have excellent systems that give them current information. This allows the owner/manager to concentrate on the "business of the business" rather than in the business.

Good systems are key in the successful day-to-day operation of businesses.

Good systems allow a business to easily expand and allow you to take a much needed break from your business.

A system is a collection of processes and procedures.

A process is the way in which a task is undertaken from start to finish.

A procedure is a set of written instructions for replicating the process.

Your business procedures and tasks should all be documented.

The main benefits of documenting all procedures and tasks are:

1. Reducing costs when training new employees.

2. Keeping current staff performance up.

3. Reducing risk when a key staff member leaves or is sick.

4. Keeping consistency. Your team needs to be able to deliver your customers the same result consistently.

5. Allowing customers to receive a high quality level of service no matter which team member is dealing with them.

Your systems manual can be printed or electronic but needs to be kept up to date and reviewed regularly.

Compiling a systems manual is a time consuming process.

The best place to start is with the most important tasks for the operation of your business.

Involve your team and ask them to provide you with a list of tasks they carry out on a regular basis.

The next step is to prioritise the tasks.

Then start by breaking down each task into its parts.

Ask your team members to write down exactly how the task is currently being performed.

Review, amend for best practice and document the procedure.

Test by getting someone else to follow the procedure.

Once you are happy with the procedure then add to the procedures manual. It may also be appropriate to keep individual procedures and tools in the vicinity of where they need to be used.

For example:

Keep the phone answering checklist by the phone.

The safest way to keep your procedures is in one central, electronic place.

This means that when a procedure is updated, everyone has access instantly without having to print too many new copies.

Action plan

1. Decide on how you will store your Systems Manual.

2. Prioritise the procedures to be written.

3. Commit to writing at least one new procedure per day.

Let's now look at software for your trades business.

Software

I recommend that you invest in the best hardware and software that's available for your industry. It will save you time and money in the future

Accounting System.

We recommend Xero.com

Xero

Xero is a cloud based (online) accounting system, available wherever there is internet access and allows multiple users. With Xero you can instantly see all your bank balances, recent sales and upcoming bills. There is free online support, its mobile, has multi currency and is secure.

CRM system

The CRM system we recommend is Capsule. This is full CRM system and can be fully integrated with Xero. It's very easy to use and set up is simple.

Job management and scheduling

There are a number of great Job Management systems out there suited to different sizes and types of businesses.

Our recommendations:

SimPRO

simPRO comes loaded with features that make running your business a breeze. simPRO understand how business works in the trade contracting industry. So in consultation with hundreds of contractors, they have developed and refined modules to make every step in the process simple. And keep your business profitable.

simPRO makes estimating quicker and easier for any sized project. Fire off quotes with the confidence that your prices are accurate and up-to-date.

simPRO's objective is to keep your cash flow, well, flowing. Your admin staff can easily manage and maintain your margins on each job. They get instant visibility into estimated profits vs actual profits, even before the invoice is raised.

simPRO keeps your schedules on track. You can schedule staff and transfer labour costs directly to any job. You can also dispatch tasks wirelessly to field staff and know instantly when it's been accepted.

simPRO puts you in the driver's seat. Your material and labour costs are directly assigned to individual projects, giving you instant visibility on actual costs at any stage of the project

simPRO makes it smooth and seamless – order parts from within jobs, and raise purchase orders at your best discounts. Access real-time stock levels from every storage location – including back orders and overdue POs for jobs. You'll dramatically reduce revisits to wholesalers, keeping your staff onsite and making money.

simPRO let's you stay ahead of that ever-growing list of assets you need to maintain for your clients. With proactive servicing schedules and alerts, you'll always be in control.

simPRO keeps your business mean, lean and super responsive. Now the data can be entered in real-time in the field, the moment it's done. That effectively removes the processing bottlenecks between completed job cards and issuing invoices. And that means faster billing and improved cash flow.

simPRO works hand in hand with your Accounting software, to eliminate double data entry and keep both systems up to date.

simPRO makes it simple to maintain a satisfied customer base and keep those regular, easy-margin jobs ticking over smoothly.

To view case studies:

- For Multi company - Plumbquick and Allied - http://simpro.co/blog/case-studies/plumbquick-and-allied-plumbing-case-study/

- The Benefits of simPRO to create Effecient Buisness - http://simpro.co/blog/case-studies/the-benefits-of-simpro-in-creating-an-efficient-business/

- simPRO and Xero - seamless integration - http://simpro.co/blog/accounting/simpro-and-xero-seamless-integration/

Geoop

If you have a mobile workforce (2-100 staff on the road) then look at Geoop. GeoOP is an award winning Cloud-based job management solution for businesses with mobile employees.

GeoOP streamlines business processes such as job scheduling, quotes, time and materials tracking, invoicing (via popular accounting systems) and inventory (via Unleashed).

It supports popular platforms such as iPhone, iPad and Android phones and tablets. Put simply, GeoOP connects your operations managers and field staff and streamlines your job management.

Website: www.geoop.com

To view case studies: http://www.geoop.com/compass-gas-and-plumbing

For a smaller business we would recommend Job Sheet.

JobSheet

What it does

Jobsheet is a complete system for tracking jobs, quoting, recording time & materials, and invoicing.

Record customers details including multiple properties

- Add notes to customer cards for easy reference to past events
- See all jobs notes made about the customer
- See all history of jobs
- View all properties

Create new jobs & assign to a tradesman

- Simple job card format just like you would do on paper
- Schedule job & see current schedule

Schedule jobs & book in with a tradesman

- Have the option to schedule or leave 'open' for when a particular tradesman or a team member can do the job
- Manage & update from the office or out on the road on behalf of the customer at any time

Create quotes & estimates on site

- Email quotes & estimates to the customer directly from on site
- Easily see what quotes are not confirmed, and follow up
- See all pricing and margins from the customer's property which means you can do a proper quote on site with no paperwork required back at the office later

Record time & materials

- Create sections for each part of the job – eg. Kitchen, Bathroom etc and track each section's labour & materials
- All price books you need are at your fingertips with buy & sell prices
- Easy to use and fast to find products you want

Invoice

- Set who can invoice the work
- See a list of all jobs that need invoicing / approving by those who have the permission to do so
- Link the invoice directly with your Xero account (no double entry)
- Flexible formatting for showing or hiding what you want the customer to see

Set permissions for your staff

- What jobs they can see -- everyone's or just their own
- Information such as what invoices are waiting payment can be locked
- Buy price from price books can be hidden
- Who can invoice, and who can just complete the work
... and more

Payroll

We would recommend something easy to use and mobile. For New Zealand readers we would suggest Smart Payroll. www.smartpayroll.co.nz

Other systems:

Debtor Management:

Make sure you get paid on time.

Make sure you invoice as soon as the job is complete. If you don't invoice on time then you are running a charity not a business. Cloud software allows you to invoice while on the job and in many cases receive payment immediately.

Put in place systems so that you can consistently follow up on all clients who owe you money.

Look at SmartAR (for NZ tradies) or Debtor Daddy (International) as options.

Terms of trade

Make sure you have written and signed terms of trade before doing business with anyone. Get professional help to get contracts drafted for your business.

Terms of trade can range from a one page document to a more complex document many pages long.

Terms of trade can often be found printed on the reverse of invoices.

The customer should accept your terms before the goods or services are provided. If they do not sign acceptance of your terms, then they could later claim they did not know about them or agree to them.

Ask your accountant to help you with your terms of trade or email businessbuddy@astillhawke.co.nz for a FREE Guide on Terms of Trade.

Action plan

1.   Review or set up your terms of trade in conjunction with your accountant.

2.   Contact Astill Hawke & Associates Ltd businessbuddy@astillhawke.co.nz for your FREE Terms of Trade Guide.

Now let's take a look at the numbers.

Financials

It's very important that you understand your numbers.

First thing to do is make sure that you get your pricing right. This can be a complex area.

Pricing

You need to make sure that you don't underprice as this will reduce profits, but at the same time, overpricing for labour and material mark-ups could turn your customers away.

Setting charge out rates is just as important as market awareness, product development and advertising. You can do all these things excellently and then undo the lot by setting charge out rates too low or too high.

Pricing is a complex strategy which should be carefully undertaken and reviewed.

Know Your Overheads

First of all you must know what it costs you to operate your business before you start to set a charge-out rate. Your accountant can help you prepare this information. In particular, you'll need to look at:

- Annual budget
- Budget for investment in stock, work in progress and debtors
- Cash-flow forecast.

It would also be a good idea to start producing periodic accounting reports, say monthly, so you can check how the business is going compared to the budget.

Customers Don't Choose on Price Alone

Once you've worked out your bottom line, don't simply jump in with the lowest rate. There is no doubt that charge-out rates are of concern to customers but contrary to what you might think, they are not the only thing customers take into account when choosing a tradesperson.

Far from it. In fact astute customers tend to choose tradespeople primarily for reliability. Other factors which enter into the buying decision include:

- Quality
- Technical and back-up services
- Reputation
- Punctuality – turning up on time!
- Tidiness
- Location
- Guarantees
- Refund policy

It would help to do some research on what goes into your customers' buying decisions before setting your rates. For example, looking at what your competitors do and how they charge could be one way of determining what customers in your area are looking for.

Do your competitors offer round-the-clock and/or prompt service, do they give guarantees or are they renowned for quality work? If they are flat-out busy yet charge a high rate, chances are customers care more about the service than the money they have to spend.

In the market place you'll find many businesses charging 5%, 10% and 20% higher than their competitors, yet still run very profitable businesses. In fact these businesses are often the most successful because they have achieved excellence in those areas listed above.

Just a word on discounting.

Discounting

The following table indicates the increase in sales required to compensate for a price discounting policy. For example, if your gross margin is 30% and you reduce price by 10% you need sales volume to increase by 50% to maintain your profit. Rarely has such a strategy worked in the past and it's unlikely that it will work in the future.

If your present gross profit rate is:

	5%	10%	15%	20%	25%	30%	35%	40%	45%	50%	55%	60%
And you reduce your price by:	To produce the same profit your sales must increase by:											
2%	67%	25%	15%	11%	9%	7%	6%	5%	5%	4%	4%	3%
4%	400%	67%	36%	25%	19%	15%	13%	11%	10%	9%	8%	7%
6%		150%	67%	43%	32%	25%	21%	18%	15%	14%	12%	11%
8%		400%	114%	67%	47%	36%	30%	25%	22%	19%	17%	15%
10%			200%	100%	67%	50%	40%	33%	29%	25%	22%	20%
12%			400%	150%	92%	67%	52%	43%	36%	32%	28%	25%
14%				233%	127%	88%	67%	54%	45%	39%	34%	30%
16%				400%	178%	114%	84%	67%	55%	47%	41%	36%
18%				900%	257%	150%	106%	82%	67%	56%	49%	43%
20%					400%	200%	133%	100%	80%	67%	57%	50%
25%						500%	250%	167%	125%	100%	83%	71%
30%							600%	300%	200%	150%	120%	100%

Increasing your price

If you adopt a premium pricing strategy the following table shows the amount by which your sales would have to decline following a price increase before your gross profit is reduced below its present level. For example, at a 40% margin, a 10% increase in price could sustain a 20% reduction in sales volume.

If your present gross profit rate is:

	5%	10%	15%	20%	25%	30%	35%	40%	45%	50%	55%	60%
And you incr ease your pric e by:	**To produce the same profit your sales may reduce by:**											
2%	29%	17%	12%	9%	7%	6%	5%	5%	4%	4%	4%	3%
4%	44%	29%	21%	17%	14%	12%	10%	9%	8%	7%	7%	6%
6%	55%	38%	29%	23%	19%	17%	15%	13%	12%	11%	10%	9%
8%	62%	44%	35%	29%	24%	21%	19%	17%	15%	14%	13%	12%
10%	67%	50%	40%	33%	29%	25%	22%	20%	18%	17%	15%	14%
12%	71%	55%	44%	38%	32%	29%	26%	23%	21%	19%	18%	17%
14%	74%	58%	48%	41%	36%	32%	29%	26%	24%	22%	20%	19%

16%	76%	62%	52%	44%	39%	35%	31%	29%	26%	24%	23%	21%
18%	78%	64%	55%	47%	42%	38%	34%	31%	29%	26%	25%	23%
20%	80%	67%	57%	50%	44%	40%	36%	33%	31%	29%	27%	25%
25%	83%	71%	62%	56%	50%	45%	42%	38%	36%	33%	31%	29%
30%	86%	75%	67%	60%	55%	50%	46%	43%	40%	38%	35%	33%

Know your breakeven point

This is the point where you do not make a loss but you also don't make a profit. You need to know this in order to cost and quote accurately.

Here is our Business Buddy Breakeven Point Calculator to allow you to calculate your breakeven point.

A company's break-even point is the amount of sales or revenues that it must generate in order to equal its expenses

Formula = $\dfrac{\text{total expenses}}{\text{gross profit \%}}$ * $\dfrac{100}{1}$

Breakeven calculation (mark-up percentage)

Calculate the necessary level of sales based on profit margin %

Total fixed and variable expenses	A	
Average profit margin on products sold	B	
Required sales level per year (divide by 52 for weekly)	A/B	$ -

Breakeven calculation (unit margin)

Calculate the necessary level of sales based on the profit on a product. This method can also be used when you charge out by the hour

Total fixed and variable expenses	A	
Profit on each item sold (or hour worked)	B	
Required sales level - units (or hours) per year	A/B	0

Now let's look at your Gross Profit.

Gross Profit

Remember your gross margin is the difference between the price of your service and what it costs you to provide it.

It is usually easier (although not always) to increase price than reduce cost.

Many tradespeople refuse to charge a high enough price and therefore make enough profit. You are not in business to match the price your competitors set, you are there to service your customers.

It's very important to view your GP% at the end of every week and month and take action where required for any variances.

Now let's take a look at Markup vs Margin.

Mark up vs. margin

I am confident that there are plenty of tradespeople who do not understand the difference and are therefore not as profitable as they think.

Two terms are used when discussing prices - markup and margin.   They are different ways of calculating profit and the difference is not often understood.

Many tradespeople use markup which is not the same as margin.

Margin

The percentage margin is the percentage of the final selling price that is profit.

Markup

Markup - the percentage of the cost price you add on to get the selling price.

Example

An example is if a job costs $100 and is priced at $150.

Markup = to get a 50% mark up is 100+(50%*100) = $150.

But this is where it can be confusing - a 50% mark up is not a 50% margin. Margin is what shows your profitability.

Margin = (price-cost)/price so in this example (150-100)/150 = 33.33%

To price on margin take cost and divide by(1 - % margin you are after.) So to get a margin of 50% you would need to sell your service for $100/(1-.5) = $100/.5 = $200 not the $150 originally thought.

For a quick reference guide:

A 15% Markup = 13% Gross Profit

A 30% Markup = 23% Gross Profit

A 50% Markup = 33.3% Gross Profit

A 100% Markup = 50% Gross Profit

Benchmarking

This is where you can compare to what others in your industry are doing to determine how well you are performing and how you compare.

Benchmarks enable you to:

- compare how your business is performing against others in your industry
- Assist you with your business planning and/or budgeting
- work out if you need to review your business and record keeping practices

The benchmarks will give you a better picture of your competitive position.

Accurate data of a suitable sample size can be difficult to obtain. However many trade associations hold benchmarking data and often Government revenue departments hold data.

The following is from the New Zealand Inland Revenue Website as an example of the type of data that is available.

E3232 - Electrical services

Performance benchmarks

These performance benchmarks have been developed from financial statements and tax returns for the year 2010/2011. They are provided as ranges and mid-points (medians). The ranges have been chosen so that most businesses in an industry are within or close to the published benchmark range. Half the businesses in a turnover range will be below the mid-point, or median, and half will be above the median.

Ratio	Small $60,000-$300,000 annual turnover	Medium $300,000-$800,000 annual turnover	Large $800,000+ annual turnover
Gross Profit Ratio	56 to 87% Median 66%	50 to 68% Median 59%	46 to 66% Median 57%
Stock turnover per annum	6 to 33 times Median 15 times	10 to 47 times Median 23 times	9 to 47 times Median 19 times
Salaries and wages/turnover	0 to 44% Median 27%	23 to 40% Median 32%	22 to 39% Median 32%

This class consists of units mainly engaged in the installation of electrical wiring or fittings in buildings or other construction projects. Electrical work arising from the installation of appliances is included in this class.

Primary activities:

- Electric light installation
- Electric wiring installation
- Electrical installation work (for example switchboards, circuit breakers, etc)
- Installation of television antennae or cable
- Installation of television satellite dish
- Repair or maintenance of electrical wiring (except of electricity transmission or distribution lines)
- Telecommunication cable or wire installation (except transmission lines)
- Traffic signal installation

Action plan

1. Source benchmarking data for your industry

2. Measure your business against this data

3. Take action where required

If stuck contact your accountant.

Now lets move on to KPI's.

KPI's

A key performance indicator (KPI) is a measure designed to track critical success factors in a business.

KPIs provide a statistical measure of how well an organisation is doing.

KPIs differ by industry, business and even departments within a business.

Whichever KPIs are selected, they must reflect the business goals, they must be key to its success, and they must be quantifiable (measurable).

If a KPI is going to be of any value, there must be a way to accurately define and measure it. 'Generate more repeat customers' is useless as a KPI without some way to distinguish between new and repeat business. 'Be the most popular company' won't work as a KPI without some accurate method of establishing the company's popularity and comparing it to others.

You also need to set targets for each KPI.

Show the target for each KPI and the progress towards that target.

Here is an example of Specialist KPIs for Construction and Engineering

- **Specialist KPIs for Construction and Engineering**

KPI	Context and Measurement
% of construction raw materials recycled to other projects	Identifies reduction of wastage
Cost per square metre compared to budget	This KPI applies only to new builds and renovation projects. It is calculated by dividing the projects total cost by the total floor area
Actual construction time compared to planned construction time	This KPI should be expressed in days. You need to be clear about the construction start and finish dates. Project delays due to external factors should be deducted
Rework cost % during project	This KPI measures the cost of fixing substandard work during the project, expressed in dollars as a percentage of the contract price
Rework cost % post handover	This KPI measures the cost of fixing defects in construction after the project has been completed and handed over to the customer, expressed in dollars as a percentage of the contract price

Action plan

Determine what KPIs to use

Decide how you will measure them

Determine the frequency in which you will report.

Here is a template for your use.

KPI Selection Worksheet

KPI	Calculation Method	Reporting Frequency	Reported to

Team

You may have your marketing sorted, your systems under control and have a full and accurate picture of your financial situation but without the right team on board this may all go to waste.

You can manage you team's productivity and efficiency with the right tools and systems.

To generate wealth, you need employees to give your business critical mass and economies of scale.

Make sure you have the right systems. Use your accountant to ensure that all your documentation is in order. For New Zealand readers check out the Employer Documentation Kit http://www.astillhawke.co.nz/resources/employer_documentation _kit

About the author

Kirsten Hawke **BCom(Hons) CA**

Kirsten Hawke is a Chartered Accountant and the CEO and founder of Astill Hawke & Associates Accountants Ltd. Ever since first going into Practice in 2002, Kirsten has had the vision to create an accounting practice that focuses on its clients.

Kirsten has a strong background in business management which really helps her get to know her client's businesses and how they function. Based on her experiences and expertise, Kirsten has proven she can provide guidance in such things as human resources (getting the best out of your staff), business structuring and regular management reporting.

Kirsten currently lives in Auckland, New Zealand with her husband, two young children and their dog. Kirsten has a strong interest in helping in the community.

Astill Hawke & Associates Ltd

Astill Hawke & Associates Limited are not your standard accountants. We specialise in providing accounting and business development services to tradespeople. We care about the success of your business and understand the issues that you face.

We regularly come across tradespeople who are simply not up to date with compliance, paying too much tax and not realising the potential of their businesses.

We understand your business and can solve your compliance issues and help you to grow your business.

In 2011 we developed and launched Business Buddy to provide our clients with monthly packages to help grow their businesses.

In 2012 we launched Tradeaccountants.

www.tradeaccountants.co.nz

Resources and references

Graham McGregor

Graham McGregor is a marketing consultant and the creator of the 396 page Free 'Unfair Business Advantage Report.' www.theunfairbusinessadvantage.com. This simple marketing system has helped many businesses to grow their revenues by 10% or more over a 12 month period.

Author of Solid Gold Testimonials.

Blog

http://blog.business-buddy.co.nz/

Facebook

http://www.facebook.com/YourTradeBiz

Twitter

@astillhawke

Website

www.tradeaccountant.co.nz

www.business-buddy.co.nz

www.astillhawke.co.nz

iPhone App

Great checklists and calculators

http://itunes.apple.com/app/id426333031

Software Providers

www.xero.com

www.simpro.co.nz

www.jobsheetapp.com

www.geoop.com

www.capsulecrm.com

www.smartpayroll.co.nz

www.debtordaddy.com

www.howtocollectdebt.co.nz

www.ingramcontent.com/pod-product-compliance
Lightning Source LLC
Chambersburg PA
CBHW051242170526
45165CB00004B/1546